Billie Jean KING

BILLIE JEAN KING
Tennis Star & Social Activist

by Marty Gitlin

Content Consultant:
Randy Walker, tennis historian

Published by ABDO Publishing Company, 8000 West 78th Street, Edina, Minnesota 55439. Copyright © 2011 by Abdo Consulting Group, Inc. International copyrights reserved in all countries. No part of this book may be reproduced in any form without written permission from the publisher. SportsZone™ is a trademark and logo of ABDO Publishing Company.

Printed in the United States of America,
North Mankato, Minnesota
112010
012011

Editor: Rebecca Rowell
Copy Editor: Paula Lewis
Series Design: Christa Schneider
Cover Production: Christa Schneider
Interior Production: Sarah Carlson and Carol Castro

Library of Congress Cataloging-in-Publication Data
Gitlin, Marty.
 Billie Jean King : tennis star and social activist / by Marty Gitlin.
    p. cm. — (Legendary athletes)
 Includes bibliographical references and index.
 ISBN 978-1-61714-757-9
 1. King, Billie Jean—Juvenile literature. 2. Tennis players—United States—Biography—Juvenile literature. 3. Women tennis players—United States—Biography—Juvenile literature. I. Title.
 GV994.K56G58 2011
 796.342092—dc22
 [B]
                              2010046584

TABLE OF CONTENTS

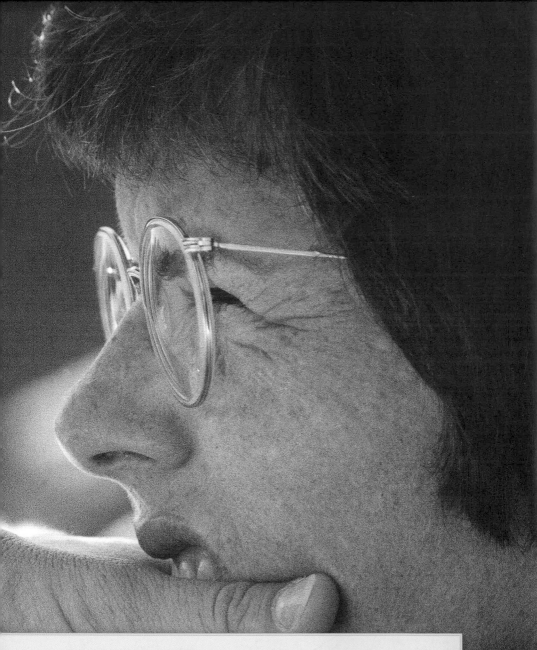

CHAPTER 1

Billie Jean King in 1972

The Mother's Day Massacre

The eyes of the tennis world were often on Billie Jean King, but not on May 13, 1973. King was finishing a tournament in Japan, but her heart and mind were in California. There, fellow tennis star Margaret Court was playing an exhibition match against Bobby Riggs. Nearly twice her age, the former tennis champion had challenged Court to a showdown. His publicity stunt exploded into a nationally televised event.

The implications were enormous. It was the height of the women's liberation movement. Women were struggling to gain equality throughout the United States, particularly in the workplace.

King was at the forefront of that battle. She was fighting for comparable pay for female tennis players. She had passionately backed Title IX, a bill signed by President Richard Nixon in 1972 that ensured equal federal funding for women's sports in high schools and colleges. She also had led the campaign to launch a professional tennis tour for women. Court's defeat by the 55-year-old Riggs would be a setback for King and all she had worked for.

So, when King boarded a plane for Los Angeles, California, she asked a flight attendant if she had heard the result of the Court-Riggs match. King was eager to learn who had won the match. When the jet landed at an airport for a layover in Hawaii, King and fellow tennis star Rosie Casals found a coin-operated television set in a waiting area. The women dropped a few quarters in and switched through the channels, but their search was fruitless. All they could find were reruns of the popular television show *Gunsmoke*.

Viewing the Riggs-Court Match

King did not have an opportunity to watch the Riggs-Court showdown until the night before she was to play Riggs. King felt that Riggs had won the mental battle right away when he presented Court with a bouquet of roses and wished her a happy Mother's Day. Court curtsied when she received the flowers, which King saw as a sign that she had little intensity and was not passionate enough about trying to win.

Shocking News

Finally, they heard news of the event over Casals's radio. It was not good. Riggs had dominated Court in two lopsided sets, winning 6–2, 6–1. The match had lasted only 57 minutes. It became known as the Mother's Day Massacre.

King was devastated. The tennis star's anger grew as she walked through the airport terminal. Her mind took a leap back to several months earlier when Riggs had sent telegrams to Court, Chris Evert, and King, challenging the women to a tennis match. Although he had contacted Court and Evert, Riggs really wanted to play King, goading her by calling the tennis star, "The sex leader of the revolutionary pack."[1] But she had achieved greatness on the tennis court, so the match was not all about her anymore. She did not feel accepting a confrontation with Riggs would in any way benefit women's tennis, so she declined his offer to play.

Little did King know that when she rejected the offer, Riggs would move on to Court. One day, King and Court shared an elevator during a tournament in Detroit, Michigan. That is when King received the stunning news:

> "I'm going to play Bobby Riggs," Margaret mentioned. . . .
> "What?"
> "I'm getting ten thousand dollars."
> "That's not enough," Billie countered, "and, secondly, this is not about tennis."
> "What do you mean? I'm about to get ten thousand dollars."
> "Margaret, I'm just going to ask one thing of you: You have to win this match." Margaret nodded politely. Too politely.
> "No, I mean it. You have to win this match. You have no idea how important this is."[2]

King was right—Court had no idea how important the match was. Court thought of Riggs as a harmless hustler simply attempting to make a buck. But the challenge meant more to Riggs than a means to steal the spotlight. He had been complaining that older tennis players competing on the senior circuit deserved more prize money. Meanwhile, he was belittling King and others for claiming that female players should be paid the same as the male players. The outgoing,

King versus Court

King and Court boasted similar strengths in tennis. Both could play with power and win with fast serves and skills that put opponents away at the net. But their similarities ended with regard to personality and a passion for women's rights. King used her confidence and outgoing nature to push for equality between the sexes; Court was reserved and not politically involved. While King and others were battling to ensure equal prize money and establish a separate tour for female players, Court remained on the sideline.

King believed Court accepted the challenge match from Riggs strictly for the money and his badmouthing of women did not bother her. That view was explained in a biography of King:

Margaret just wasn't the defiant type. She was more introverted than her [outspoken] peers; someone who usually minimized her presence. . . . She didn't enjoy standing out or speaking up. . . . To her, a bank of microphones looked about as friendly as a gang of alien invaders.[3]

Court's loss to Riggs did not affect her play. Despite being 31, which is old for competing tennis players, she was ranked No. 1 in the world in 1973 after winning three of the four major professional tennis events.

boastful Riggs was certainly not one to turn down a second chance at fame. And he firmly believed that even an aging former champion such as himself could defeat the best women tennis players in the world, including King.

Showdown Inevitable

After his domination of Court, Riggs was cockier than ever—and King was angrier than ever. The moment she heard that Riggs had won, King knew what she had to do. She had to play him and beat him. The future of both the women's equality movement and women's tennis depended on it.

Riggs could have claimed that he made his point by winning the match against Court and then fade into obscurity. But he saw an opportunity to make a financial killing. He wasted no time and challenged King as he spoke to the media following his defeat of Court. He boasted that he could beat King on any tennis surface:

> Now I want King bad. I'll play her on clay, grass, wood, cement, marble, or roller skates. We got to keep this sex thing going. I'm a woman specialist now.[4]

King knew all about Riggs, who was a local hero where she grew up in Southern California. Riggs performed brilliantly as a tennis player in the 1930s and 1940s. He won the Wimbledon triple crown in 1939, taking all events he entered at the All England Lawn Tennis Club: singles, doubles, and mixed doubles. After turning professional, which, at the time, made him ineligible for Wimbledon and the other Grand Slam tournaments, Riggs continued to excel. He won the US Pro Championship in 1946, 1947, and 1949 and was recognized as the best professional tennis player in the world.

As King honed her own tennis skills as a child, she had admired Riggs's talent. But King was not a child anymore, and she knew she had to avenge Court's defeat. She accepted the challenge and told Riggs that their showdown would be a one-time event. She made it clear to her opponent that they would never play against each other again. Riggs agreed; the Battle of the Sexes was on.

The match was scheduled for September 20, 1973. A winner's check of $100,000 was at stake. It was the largest amount ever paid for a tennis match. To King, there was much more at stake. After all, she would be playing for women everywhere. There would be enormous pressure. But Billie Jean King was used to playing under pressure. She had been playing on behalf of others since the magical moment when she swung a tennis racket for the first time.

Riggs presented Court, *left*, with a bouquet of red roses just before the start of their tennis match. The move was intended to disarm her.

CHAPTER 2

Long Beach, California, Billie Jean's hometown

California Tomboy

Billie Jean Moffitt was born on November 22, 1943, in Long Beach, California. She was the first of two children in her middle-class family. Her brother, Randy, was born five years later. Billie Jean's father, Bill Moffitt, was a firefighter. Her mother, Betty Moffitt, was a homemaker.

Billie Jean grew up in a sports-crazed household. Her father loved to play, watch, listen to, and talk about sports. Quite athletic, Bill Moffitt had played basketball in the US Navy and even competed once against legendary baseball player Jackie Robinson. The National Basketball Association invited Moffitt to a tryout, but he turned it down. He opted for a more conventional job and the steady paycheck that went along with it.

Billie Jean developed her own passion for sports and became a tomboy. She liked playing softball and played touch football with the neighborhood boys. She even dreamed of playing for the NFL's Green Bay Packers one day.

Though she was outside playing sports quite often, Billie Jean admitted that she could sit still for her favorite television shows. The medium of television was fairly new to Americans at that time.

Introduction to Tennis

When she was 11 years old, Billie Jean was introduced to a new sport. She was in the fifth grade classroom of her elementary school, listening to her teacher, Mrs. Delph. She was sitting next to Susan Williams, one of her new best friends.

Then, one simple question uttered by the girl from the desk across the aisle changed Billie Jean's life forever. She wrote about the event as an adult:

Susan was a brilliant girl and one of my closest friends, but that was not the only reason she was so important in my life. One day in class, she asked me:

Mom's Baking

Betty Moffitt sold Tupperware and Avon products out of their home to help contribute to the household income, and she was quite adept at domestic chores. Billie Jean recalled with fondness her mother baking batches of tasty cookies in the afternoon. Billie Jean would grab them as she went in and out of the house. Billie Jean also enjoyed her mom's pumpkin chiffon pie.

"Do you want to play tennis?"
A simple question, but one that would have a
profound impact on me.
"What's tennis?" I replied.
"You get to run, jump and hit a ball," Susan said.
Those were my three most favorite things to do, so
I said, "Sure, I'll try it!"[1]

Billie Jean joined Susan that weekend and played tennis for the first time.

Pursuing Tennis

After her first experience on a tennis court with Susan, Billie Jean decided she wanted to play again. Through her softball coach, Billie Jean discovered that Clyde Walker, an instructor with the Long Beach Parks and Recreation Department, was giving free lessons once a week. She was excited at a chance to play more regularly.

Walker made the sport fun for Billie Jean. She laughed and ran and learned basics such as how to grip the racket and hit the ball. It took just one session to hook Billie Jean on the sport. When her mother came to pick her up, Billie Jean claimed to her mother with all seriousness that she was going to be the

A Love of Music

As a child, Billie Jean loved listening to big band music. Her parents were huge fans of the genre and often played records. The couple particularly enjoyed the works of highly popular bandleader Glenn Miller. Sometimes, Billie Jean's parents spent their free time ballroom dancing to big band music.

No. 1 tennis player in the world someday.

Her First Racket

Billie Jean was so motivated to play tennis that she scoured the neighborhood for odd jobs to earn enough money to buy a racket of her own. She took out the trash, worked in gardens, and saved the money. When she had saved $8.29, a hefty sum for children in the 1950s, Billie Jean begged her mother to drive her to the sporting goods store. Young Billie Jean discovered to her delight that her earnings were enough to purchase a wood racket with purple strings and grip—her favorite color.

Billie Jean's parents might have chuckled at their daughter's claim that she would blossom into the best player in the world, but they loved the fact that she was going to work toward that

Randy Moffitt

When Billie Jean was 11 years old, she attended a minor league baseball game with her brother, Randy. She turned to him during the game and exclaimed, "You can be a big-league ballplayer and I can't." When he asked why, she replied, "Because I'm a girl."[2]

Randy Moffitt did become a big-league ballplayer. He was a first-round draft pick of the San Francisco Giants in 1970 and played with that team for ten years. During that time, he developed into one of the best relief pitchers in baseball. Moffitt arguably performed his best in 1973, the year his sister played Bobby Riggs in the Battle of the Sexes. In that season, he established himself with 14 saves. He was responsible for at least 11 saves in each of the next five years.

Billie Jean was always proud of her brother and his achievements. She enjoyed being introduced as Randy Moffitt's sister.

Billie Jean's discovery of tennis as a child would change her life.

goal. They encouraged her every step of the way. Bill Moffitt placed a spotlight in the backyard so Billie Jean could practice at night. He also made certain that his daughter kept the sport in the proper perspective. After one occasion when she lost her temper on the court, he confiscated her racket and in front of her took it to the garage and turned on the power saw. She feared he was going to saw her racket in half. He did not damage Billie Jean's racket, but he clearly made the point that Billie Jean would no longer be allowed to play tennis if she did not control her anger.

Billie Jean's practice quickly paid off. She improved enough to occasionally participate in tournaments held at the prestigious Los Angeles Tennis Club, which served as a playground for the wealthiest kids in town. While the majority of the girls competed in the most expensive skirts and dresses, Billie Jean wore homemade clothing.

Billie Jean felt that the kids of modest means were treated fine by their rich peers but not as respectfully by the adults. The president of the Southern California Lawn Tennis Association asked Billie Jean to step out when she began posing for a photo with the other players because she was wearing tennis shorts rather than a dress or skirt. From that moment on,

Being a Girl

Because she was a girl, Billie Jean faced discrimination early in life, and often from other women. Her female junior high school principal refused to sign a permission slip allowing Billie Jean to compete in a crucial event in Santa Monica, the Dudley Cup. Billie Jean cried and cajoled her until the principal gave in and reluctantly signed the slip. Billie Jean later wrote about the event, "She took no pride whatsoever that one of her students might bring the school some recognition and honor."[3]

Billie Jean knew she had to change things. She wrote about the experience later:

> Ever since that day when I was eleven years old and I wasn't allowed in a photo because I wasn't wearing a tennis skirt, I knew I wanted to change the sport.[4]

Lesson Learned

Billie Jean's family did not belong to a country club. The Moffitts were not wealthy. Theirs was a typical middle-class American home of the 1950s. Her father went out to work while her mother ran the house and raised the kids.

But there was one distinction about her family that struck Billie Jean. Her father shared the housework with his wife when he returned home from work. And her mother worked to earn money whenever possible.

Billie Jean cherished the fact that a man and woman could work so well together and that their jobs were not so clearly defined. The memories of her parents and of experiences at the country club would serve Billie Jean well later in life. They would also motivate her to fight to change the traditional roles of men and women in the United States and to work toward making tennis popular for everyone.

To do these things, Billie Jean would have to make a name for herself, which she did by improving

"It's each generation's job to push the next."[5]
—*Billie Jean King*

dramatically. She studied the game and soaked in every bit of knowledge she could while working on her skills. Soon, her prediction that she would be the best player in the world did not seem so far-fetched.

Billie Jean's first racket would have been made of wood, unlike the rackets used by tennis players today.

CHAPTER 3

Alice Marble played at Wimbledon in June 1937.

Marble, Wimbledon, and College

Billie Jean had to battle more than opponents on the court to pursue her dream of becoming the top female tennis player in the world. She had to fight her economic reality as well. The Moffitts simply could not afford the travel expenses to out-of-state tournaments that could test Billie Jean's skills and improve her game.

So, Billie Jean did the next best thing. She began taking lessons from former champion and tennis legend Alice Marble. She not only honed Billie Jean's talents, she also imparted a strong advocacy of women's rights that stayed with her protégé for the rest of her life. At that time, girls were often discouraged from participating in sports. Marble spent much of her life encouraging them.

Billie Jean's parents drove their daughter 40 miles (65 km) every Saturday and let Marble work with her the entire weekend. Marble entertained her student with stories about her experiences as the No. 1 player in the world. The two developed a rapport both on and off the court.

Marble fascinated Billie Jean with her reminiscences of the past. She also transformed Billie Jean into a dominating player at the net. While other young players hit strictly from the baseline, Billie Jean learned to rush in and put away volleys, balls hit on the fly, just as Marble had done a generation earlier.

Losing Marble

The relationship between Billie Jean and Marble was not always easy. It began unraveling when Billie Jean announced to Marble that she wanted to be the best player ever. Her instructor reacted negatively.

Billie Jean believed Marble took the statement as a pronouncement that she wanted to be better than her.

And on one occasion, Marble became angered when she informed Billie Jean that she was too sick to teach that day and the young teenager responded rudely. Billie Jean's parents made her apologize, but afterward, Marble quit as Billie Jean's instructor, which led

Strong Beliefs

A well-rounded teenager, Billie Jean grew up in a fairly religious home. She attended church every Sunday and she read the Bible every night before going to sleep. She participated in an organization called Youth for Christ at her school. At one point in her childhood, she yearned to become a missionary and spread the beliefs of Christianity to other people.

Billie Jean to a period of self-examination.

Former tennis champion Maureen Connolly reacted the same way as Marble when Billie Jean said her goal was to be No. 1. Billie Jean was beginning to think she was indeed selfish and egotistical. She learned from the experience and began making certain that she was prepared for every match and never allowed overconfidence to seep in.

Marble had improved Billie Jean's game to the point where, at age 15, she had landed a spot on the Junior Wightman Cup team. The team competed annually against the premier players of that age group from Great Britain. Billie Jean played on the team in 1959 and 1960 and began earning enough sponsor money to play in other prestigious youth tennis events that earlier she had not

Marble's Other Talents

Billie Jean's mentor, Alice Marble, was more than a great tennis champion in her day. She also played the guitar and sang professionally. On occasion, Marble would play the guitar and sing to Billie Jean during their free time between tennis lessons. While Marble performed—sometimes singing in Spanish—Billie Jean would look through her instructor's scrapbook. Billie Jean would also look at the pictures on Marble's wall, including one that showed her singing in a club at a New York hotel.

been able to afford. By the middle of 1960, Billie Jean had skyrocketed to fourth in the rankings among all American female tennis players.

Winner at Wimbledon

A year later, Billie Jean missed her graduation ceremony at Long Beach Polytechnic High School to play doubles with partner Karen Hantze at the prestigious Wimbledon Championships in England.

Wimbledon

Tennis, for the most part, began as an indoor sport in France during the thirteenth century and quickly made its way to England. Originally, there were no rackets: Players hit the ball with the palms of their hands. About a 100 years later, in England, tennis caught on with the wealthy. The game was converted into an outdoor activity in 1874. The Wimbledon tennis tournament was launched three years later. Initially for men only, it was opened to women in 1884.

British players dominated Wimbledon for decades, but the growing talents of players around the world turned it into an international event by the early 1900s. Over the past 100-plus years, the host nation has only rarely produced singles or doubles champions.

The tournament is played annually over a two-week period. Wimbledon is third chronologically among the Grand Slam events. The Australian Open is held in January, the French Open is held in May, Wimbledon is held in late June and early July, and the US Open is held in late August and early September. Today, Wimbledon is the only one of the four events played on grass.

The Grand Slam event is considered by many to be the pinnacle of all tennis tournaments.

Billie Jean and Karen did not expect to get very far in their first Wimbledon experience and made reservations for flights home after the quarterfinals. They were thrilled with each victory. After winning their match, they would go out and eat hamburgers before returning to the dorm room reserved for the players for a night of giggling and stuffing themselves with candy bars.

Billie Jean and Karen were kids in an adult environment, but they did not play like kids. They played in the championship match against Australians Margaret Smith and Jan Lehane. Soon, Billie Jean and Karen celebrated victory.

Billie Jean expected a hero's welcome upon returning to the United States. To her disappointment, hardly a word of congratulations was uttered by anyone. In addition, upon her arrival, Billie Jean learned that her first tennis coach, Clyde Walker, had died of cancer. He lived long enough to know she had won at Wimbledon and was

An Early Prize

When Billie Jean began winning tennis tournaments, the trophies and other prizes accumulated. She would hand them over to her parents and forget about them. Billie Jean received a radio for winning an event in 1957. She gave it to her father, who put it in the garage that he had built himself as an addition to the house. In her autobiography that was published 25 years later, Billie Jean wrote that she suspected the radio was still in that garage.

thrilled with her victory. Billie Jean was happy with her win, but even as she decided to start college, her mind was focused on winning the singles tournament someday.

Off to College

In the fall of 1961, Billie Jean began her 18-mile (29-km) daily commute to Los Angeles State College in the used 1950 Ford she had purchased for $310.

She eventually started earning money as a playground instructor and as an attendant, handing out equipment and towels at the school gymnasium. She had, at least temporarily, put tennis behind her.

One day, Billie Jean's friend introduced her to a handsome young student with blue eyes and blond hair. She became mesmerized by his intelligence. They soon began dating steadily.

He would make Billie Jean think about everything in life and change her forever. His name was Larry King.

"When the day comes that a woman who is athletic will no longer be regarded as the unusual type, . . . when it will seem as natural for women as it now seems for me to be keenly interested in athletics, we'll start training girls to be active athletes. We'll not discourage them, as we do today, from taking part in tomboy play when they're six, and ten, and twelve."[2]

—*Alice Marble*

Larry King gives Billie Jean a celebratory kiss after she won a match in 1967.

CHAPTER 4

Billie Jean and Larry King on their wedding day

Finding Love

When Billie Jean began dating Larry King in 1961, she experienced someone quite different than her friends and family. She had never met anyone like Larry. She had been raised in a middle-class neighborhood by conservative, religious parents. The Moffitts were typical of many families in the 1950s. They rarely discussed the world beyond their suburban Long Beach home.

But Larry was different. He grew up in a poor area of Dayton, Ohio, before moving with his family to California. His mother had died when he was a child. Sometimes, he had no more on his dinner plate than garbanzo beans. His father raised him with a strong sense of right and wrong. On one occasion, when Larry was about seven years old, his family drove 90 miles (145 km) to Big Bear Lake in California for a family reunion. They were eager to partake in fun and games with family members they had not seen in quite some time. But when they reached the campsite, the Kings encountered a sign that read, "No Blacks Allowed."[1]

Larry's father refused to enter. He turned his car around and drove home, much to the dismay of his son. Larry later realized that it took great conviction on his father's part to not patronize a place that would not allow his fellow humans to enter. Larry began to question and form opinions about what was happening in American society. And he would eventually impart his wisdom to his new girlfriend.

Red Socks

Billie Jean could thank tennis friend Marcos Carriedo for setting her up with her future husband, Larry King. Billie Jean had been departing a library elevator when Carriedo stopped her in her tracks. Carriedo was the top player on the school's men's tennis team. He was also Billie Jean's mixed-doubles partner. He informed her that there was a young man on the third floor of the library who would be a perfect match for her. Carriedo added that the guy he wanted to introduce Billie Jean to did not drink or smoke, and he loved tennis.

Billie Jean dismissed her friend. But Carriedo insisted that Billie Jean return to the elevator and head to the third floor with him to see what he believed would be her ideal mate. When Billie Jean saw Larry, she was taken aback by his good looks.

There was only one problem: he was wearing red socks that she later described as "bright enough to lead Santa's sleigh."[1] Though Billie Jean thought that was rather strange, she approached Larry and began speaking to him. Carriedo was right. The two were a great match.

Billie Jean soon fell in love with him, and the feeling was mutual. Larry wanted her to accompany him wherever he went at school, even to the chemistry lab. But he would not allow her to abandon her tennis talent. He encouraged Billie Jean to continue playing despite the inequities between male and female athletes and how they were received in the United States. While he prodded her, she embraced his sense of justice and insight on political and social matters.

One of the most pressing issues of the 1960s and 1970s was civil rights. Black people, particularly in the South, were still fighting for their equal rights. Billie Jean's awakening to those struggles planted the seed for her realization that women in the United States faced discrimination as well. Though she was not among

Learning from Ballet Dancers

King has claimed that tennis players and other athletes could learn a great deal about balance from watching premier dancers perform, particularly ballet dancers. For that reason, she watched the movie *The Turning Point*, a film about ballet dancing, 12 times.

the first to join the growing women's movement in the early 1960s, she did begin to wonder about the inequities between women and men in tennis and in others aspects of society.

No Scholarship for Billie Jean

One example of inequality revolved around college athletic scholarships. Larry pointed out to Billie Jean that he received a scholarship to play tennis at the school even though he was not a starter on the men's team:

> I'm the seventh man on a six-man team . . . but why do I get the grant and you don't? I'm a boy. You're the biggest name at the school, and you can't get anything because you're a girl.[2]

Larry understood and encouraged equality for women. He prodded her to think about such unfairness and urged her to maximize her tennis potential. Billie Jean had lost her motivation to play tennis in a male-dominated sport where women were treated as second-class citizens. He told her in no uncertain terms that anyone as talented as she was should try to prove that she was the best in the world.

A New Coach

In 1964, Billie Jean decided to take time off from college and improve her game. She went to Australia and began training with highly respected Australian coach Mervyn Rose. Larry, who proposed to Billie Jean just before she left on her trip, encouraged her to go. He agreed with Billie Jean that this would be the only way she would ever be number one in the sport she loved.

Rose overhauled Billie Jean's game. He changed her serve and forehand. The revamped style took time for Billie Jean to master. She took steps backward before taking steps forward. She lost to players she never would have lost to before. However, the altered style eventually made Billie Jean a far better player. She reached the women's singles final of the 1965 US National Championships—known as the US Open today—but then Billie Jean lost to Margaret Smith, the future Mrs. Margaret Court.

Althea Gibson

King is a great believer in visualization, which is picturing positive things happening in one's mind. One woman who inspired her to use visualization was former tennis champion Althea Gibson, who became the first African American to win a Grand Slam event. Gibson won the French Open women's singles title in 1956 and went on to win two Wimbledon and two US singles titles. In Gibson's 1958 autobiography, *I Always Wanted to Be Somebody*, she spoke about fulfilling her dreams against all odds.

Larry was very supportive of Billie Jean and her tennis career.

Wedding Bells for Billie Jean

A few days after that 1965 US women's singles
final, on September 17, Larry and Billie Jean wed. From
then on, she would be known as Billie Jean King. Billie
Jean had persuaded Larry to go to law school, which
meant there was little money for the young couple
to live on. She earned eight dollars an hour teaching
tennis, which was against the rules for amateur players,
but she took that chance.

During the 1960s, the top tennis players were all amateurs, which meant they were not paid for their performance and received money from sports associations only for expenses. A professional tour run by promoters did exist, but it was second-rate tennis.

Those who ran the sport believed amateurs competed for the love of the game rather than for money. But often, tournament directors would secretly pay the best players to lure them to their particular events. Billie Jean was among those getting such money, but she still did not like the system.

Billie Jean knew she had to win the Wimbledon women's singles championship to earn enough fame and respect to make changes in her sport and in society. And she did that in 1966. In the best-of-three-set match, Billie Jean's 6–3, 3–6,

Playing with Glasses

King excelled at tennis despite wearing glasses, which could be affected by the weather conditions. She had to ask the umpires and schedulers to not play her on days it rained since it clouded her glasses and made it difficult to see. Many fans appreciated her bespectacled appearance. King received many letters from mothers who thanked her for wearing her glasses because it helped their own daughters feel better about themselves. This was a time when contact lenses were not as common as they are today and glasses were not considered cool, especially for girls.

A Second Wimbledon Victory

King and Hantze's women's doubles victory at Wimbledon in 1961 was not a fluke. The two young women repeated their win the following year, capturing a second Wimbledon doubles championship in 1962.

6–1 victory over Maria Bueno in the final earned Billie Jean her first Wimbledon singles title at the age of 23. She won the same event the following year, in 1967, as well as the coveted US women's singles final.

Billie Jean King had become the top women's tennis player in the world. She was thrilled about that, but she was not satisfied with her life and the lot in life of women in her sport and throughout the United States. And she was ready to do something about it.

King proudly held the winner's plate after becoming the women's singles champion at Wimbledon in 1967.

CHAPTER 5

Billie Jean and Larry celebrate another win.

Taking a Stand

In today's sports world, those who have achieved the level of athletic success that King experienced in the mid-1960s would be millionaires. King barely scraped by. With her husband in law school, she attempted to fund her career on the $14-a-day allowance tournament organizers were permitted to give players and the money they paid her secretly to play in their events. With time, her distress over the state of tennis increased, and she began speaking out.

In post-match press conferences, King would cry out in favor of what was described as an "Open Era" for the sport. It would allow the major tournaments to accept professional players and let King and others begin taking a share of the profits. United States Lawn Tennis Association (USLTA) officials, including USLTA President Bob Kelleher, cringed every time King brought up the matter. During a 1967 tournament, Kelleher warned King to stop ranting about professional tennis or she would suffer the consequences.

He was referring to the prestigious Sullivan Award, an annual honor given to the premier amateur athlete in the country. Kelleher told King in no uncertain terms that she had a good chance to win it in 1967 but had to keep her mouth shut.

Kelleher was not unsympathetic. He told King to give it more time, but she had run out of patience. Just days after her conversation with him, King won the US National Championships women's singles title and continued to voice her opinion about professional tennis. She was on a mission on and off the court.

Earnings Milestones

King was the biggest attraction and best player on the Virginia Slims tour. In 1971, the year the new circuit was launched, she earned more than $100,000. It marked the first time a female athlete ever hit that milestone. King believed it was both symbolic and positive for women in the sport and in society that she surpassed that figure in earnings.

Making a Difference

King's courage, determination, and outspokenness inspired others. In November 1967, a group of the top male tennis players declared that they were turning professional, including Australian champions John Newcombe, Tony Roche, and Roy Emerson. Tennis officials pictured empty stands, wondering who would show up to watch amateur tournaments without the best players.

In response, the International Tennis Federation (ITF) opened its events to professionals. Anyone talented enough to compete could make money. Anyone talented enough to win tournaments could make a lot of money. At first, the men were offered considerably more money than the women—something Larry warned King to expect—a fact that frustrated her and one that she would challenge.

Between 1968 and 1970, women were left out of many events altogether. A number of tournaments were run for men only. And those featuring both sexes paid the male athletes an average of 11 times more than their female counterparts.

The Physical Toll of Tennis

The physical pounding that top players take on the tennis court often leads to physical problems. For King, it meant knee surgery in 1968. King spent nearly a year recovering from the operation. She remained in the hospital for a week and was in a cast for a long time thereafter.

Medical advances have dramatically shortened recovery time for today's athletes. Knee surgery most often requires no overnight hospital stay and physical therapy can usually begin the next day.

The women players sought the men's help in their cause on a number of occasions but were rejected time and again. The USLTA was asked to form a separate women's tour, but that request was also turned down.

Finally, in 1968, the National Tennis League (NTL) provided an opportunity for men and women to tour together and play events. The short-lived NTL provided an opportunity for male and female players to learn from and come to appreciate each other—even become

The NTL

The first attempt made by amateur tennis players to form a professional circuit ended quickly. The NTL lasted one year. Founded in 1968 by former top player George MacCall, the NTL included premier and legendary talents such as Rod Laver, Ken Rosewall, and Pancho Gonzalez on the men's side as well as women stars King and Rosie Casals.

The money was not bad. King signed a two-year contract with the NTL worth $80,000 and earned every penny playing a tiring tour of Europe. The players made 18 stops in 20 days, traveling in vans and sleeping in cheap hotels. The courts and locker rooms were inferior. Still, King enjoyed the experience. She became fast friends with her fellow players. The men gained a great appreciation for the tennis talents of the women, who learned some finer points of the game from the men. And when they finished playing, the players—men and women—often stopped at clubs and danced into the early morning.

The NTL did not die because it was unsuccessful. It was destroyed by the lure of World Championship Tennis, which offered far more money.

friends—but introduction of a new tour exclusively for men ended the NTL.

In 1969, Texas oil tycoon Lamar Hunt launched the World Championship Tennis (WCT) tour, which attracted many of the top players in the sport. Unfortunately for King and her fellow female tennis players, he was interested exclusively in attracting men to the WCT. And the men she had toured with and befriended on the NTL joined the WCT without supporting King and the other female players. King was dismayed by the situation. "We don't want you, that's what they told us," she recalled. "That was a profound wake-up call. I was crushed; I was devastated. I could not believe they didn't want us."[1]

A year later, King learned that the women's tournament schedule compiled by the USLTA was virtually nonexistent. The ITF had scheduled 53 tournaments, but only 19 were for women.

The prize money was no better. Women who did not at least reach the quarterfinals of an event often went home without a penny for their efforts. That year, the Pacific Southwest Open in Los Angeles offered a $12,500 prize for the men's champion and $1,500 for the women's champion. Male tennis star Manuel Santana was quoted as saying he would rather watch cattle graze than a women's tennis match.

King stretched for a ball at Wimbledon in July 1967.

A New Direction

Faced with the prospect that the world of
professional tennis was in the process of phasing
out the women's game, King and other like-minded
women players came up with a drastic plan. In 1970,
they decided to boycott the Los Angeles event and
hold one of their own in Houston, Texas. Gladys
Heldman, founder and publisher of *World Tennis*

magazine, engineered the new event. She persuaded
Joseph Cullman of the tobacco company Philip Morris
to underwrite the tournament through the Virginia
Slims brand. The prize money would be $7,500—five
times more than Pacific Southwest Open promoter Jack
Kramer was offering the women.

It was a mutiny. King and eight other top female
tennis players signed up to play the Houston event.
USLTA officials warned them not to follow through
with their plans. The organization threatened to
suspend anyone who participated in the tournament.
In a symbolic gesture of
solidarity, the women broke
away from the USLTA by signing
professional contracts for one
dollar in Houston.

The USLTA, in turn,
banned the renegade players
from women's events such as
the Wightman Cup and the
Federation Cup. It stripped
them all of their national
rankings. If not for the courage
of King and her friends, their
careers could have been ruined.
Instead, they began their
own tennis tour and an uphill

The Virginia Slims Tour

The fledgling women's
tennis tour King helped
launch in 1971 was spon-
sored by Virginia Slims,
which marketed ciga-
rettes to women with the
slogan, "You've come a
long way, baby." King did
not like the idea of the
women's movement and
the tennis tour that rep-
resented women's rights
being linked with such
a dangerous habit. But
she concluded that the
financial benefits of the
Virginia Slims sponsor-
ship were too important
to turn down.

Chris Evert

Chris Evert emerged in 1971 as the new star attraction in women's tennis. At the age of 17, she was a champion. Evert, however, felt disliked and envied by the other women on the tour. She was, after all, the first women's tennis player to receive massive publicity. King urged her fellow female players to treat Evert nicely. "Chris has really helped women's tennis," she said. "What it needs is more personalities. If any of the other girls feel jealous about the attention she's received, they should stop and think beyond their own little worlds."[2]

struggle. Aside from King and Casals, the top women remained with the USLTA, including budding 16-year-old superstar Chris Evert.

The bold move was in step with the changing times. Since the late 1960s, many women had been battling for equal rights and equal pay. King embraced the feminist movement.

The new Virginia Slims tour lost money in 1971 and 1972, but it did well enough with the fans to remain viable. The changing attitude toward women's sports in the United States, as well as the increasing popularity of women's tennis, forced the USLTA to merge with the Virginia Slims Tour in 1973 and offered an equal payment at the US Open. That year, 1973, would prove memorable for King. Two decisions would change her life personally and professionally.

In another appearance at Wimbledon, King focused on defeating her opponent. In 1973, she beat Evonne Goolagong to advance to the women's singles finals.

CHAPTER 6

King focused on her backhand during a match.

Wanted and Unwanted Attention

The lifestyle of professional athletes is not conducive to stable marriages. Travel schedules often separate athletes from their spouses for weeks or months at a time. And fame often makes athletes targets of affection from fans.

Both scenarios combined to wreak havoc with Billie Jean's personal life in the early 1970s. Not only was she forced to be separated from her husband while she played in one tournament after another, her constant battles on behalf of women's tennis drew attention away from the marriage. Larry had accompanied Billie Jean on one tour a few years earlier and was miserable. She refused to ask him to do it again. She was lonely, but she understood that Larry had his own career and was not about to give it up to travel with his wife.

Larry would join the tennis tour eventually, though not with Billie Jean. After practicing law in Hawaii for a time, he decided to work as a tennis promoter. Larry promoted Billie Jean's

A New Kind of Racket

The tennis world changed drastically as the mid-1970s approached. Not only did new stars such as Chris Evert and Jimmy Connors spark the sport, but more power was also infused into the game. One reason for the change was an advancement in tennis rackets. Many players replaced their wooden rackets with larger metal ones. Connors, who quickly became the top-ranked player in the world, was one of the first to use a metal racket. His Wilson T-2000 was the first popular metal racket for the recreational player.

tournaments from 1971 to 1973, though he was often in one city while she played in another.

In 1971, the marriage had a new stressor. Billie Jean discovered she was pregnant. Larry believed it was a woman's choice to keep the baby or have an abortion. This was two years before the US Supreme Court ruled abortions to be legal, but Billie Jean had the option of applying to a committee of doctors for approval, and she did just that. Though she knew Larry would love to have a child, she felt their marriage was not strong at this point and did not want to bring a child into it. She was drifting away from Larry.

Still the Best

King remained nearly unbeatable on the court. The women's game was gaining in popularity, particularly after teenager Chris Evert exploded onto the scene. The two squared off in one of the most highly anticipated matches in the history of the sport during the semifinals of the 1971 US Open women's singles tournament. The 16-year-old phenom entered with a winning streak of 22 matches. Perhaps the young upstart would dethrone the perennial champion.

The world soon learned that Evert could not defeat King, at least not on that day. The veteran changed her aggressive style and hit a lot of off-speed shots. That threw off Evert's rhythm, and she became flustered. After King broke Evert's serve at 3–3 in the first set, the match was all but over for the teenager. King won nine of the last 11 games to advance to the final round. Her victory over Casals there, which gave her another US Open title, was almost anticlimactic.

But King's tennis success was not matched by joy in her personal life. *Ms.* magazine, which was campaigning to make abortion legal in the United States, sent petitions to the homes of women. The petitions asked those who had sought an

Muhammad Ali

King felt a connection to another professional athlete: Muhammad Ali, the heavyweight boxing champion. King realized that Ali was an idol to blacks much as she was an idol to women. "Muhammad Ali and I had a genuine affection for each other," King wrote in an autobiography. "Whenever we would run into each other, he would whisper in my ear, 'Billie Jean King, you're the queen.' I have no idea how much he thought about how our struggles for recognition as athletes ran parallel, but I think it was definitely a part of our connection."[1]

abortion to sign them. With his wife away, Larry signed Billie Jean's name and sent it back to the magazine without telling her. Soon, the *Washington Post* revealed that Billie Jean had had an abortion. The newspaper claimed it resulted in her best season on the court and used Larry as a source.

Then, the *Los Angeles Times* ran a story about the abortion. The news program *60 Minutes* soon followed. The public and the media speculated that King had an abortion only because it was convenient to her athletic career. But she claimed that never crossed her mind. Betty Moffitt, Billie Jean's mother, told her daughter

The Issue of Abortion

Abortion has been a highly controversial issue in US history. The heated debate has revolved around a woman's right to choose whether to terminate a pregnancy. Those who are pro-choice believe it is her decision. Those who are pro-life feel that even upon conception, a fetus is a human being and abortion is murder.

Abortions were illegal in the United States from the late 1800s until January 1973. The US Supreme Court ruled in the landmark *Roe v. Wade* case that a woman could legally end her pregnancy until the fetus developed to the point where it could survive outside the mother's womb.

The decision set off a firestorm of protest that has continued to this day. A number of unsuccessful attempts have been made to overturn *Roe v. Wade* in the courts. Thousands of Americans have protested loudly, and sometimes violently, against the legality of abortions. Those on both sides of the issue have continued to work to have the president appoint justices to the Supreme Court who agree with their views.

that she had cried for three days. She asked her daughter why she did not love Larry and children.

King had no answers for her mother. She was trying to figure out her personal life. Fortunately for King, she always had a sanctuary on the tennis court. She considered quitting the sport because of all the pressures off the court, but she remained brilliant with a racket in her hand. King won the French Open, Wimbledon, and the US Open women's singles championships in 1972 to reclaim the top ranking in the world from young Australian Evonne Goolagong.

Call to Action

With the attention her personal choices were getting, the last thing King needed was more demands on her time. But when Riggs challenged her to a Battle of the Sexes, King realized she had to accept.

The match was publicized in newspapers, magazines, and on television for weeks before the event. King was peppered with questions about it before and after every match in the interim. She told the media she was simply trying to prove that women players can be equally entertaining and, therefore, worthy of the same pay. King never claimed the current female players could beat their male counterparts of the same era. She knew the men had too much power in their games for the women to contend with.

This Little Piggy

When it came time for King and Riggs to play their tennis match, the promoters and television network played the gender angle to the hilt. King presented Riggs with a live piglet adorned with a big pink bow. This was because men who believed in male superiority during that era were called "chauvinist pigs."

But to the media and the nation, the match was simply the Battle of the Sexes. King had the honor of all women placed on her back. The pressure was enormous. She prepared for it with great vigor.

With an estimated 50 million Americans watching on television and 30,000 more attending the event at the Houston Astrodome, the pre-match festivities had all the glitz of a Las Vegas show. Famed and controversial sportscaster Howard Cosell hosted the television broadcast. On the court before the match, spectators were entertained by a marching band and dancers.

Thousands of King supporters rose to their feet screaming and clapping as she was carried onto the court by a quartet of male college track stars on a brightly decorated stretcher. Riggs fans roared as well as he was escorted in on a rickshaw pulled by several beautiful young women.

As they warmed up, King understood that Riggs was playing to promote himself and make money, while she was playing for the cause of women's equality. The burden she felt was overwhelming.

King, *foreground*, was determined to defeat Riggs in their tennis match in the Houston Astrodome in 1973.

CHAPTER 7

Riggs, *left*, and King joked a month before their big match.

Career High and Personal Low

As King entered the Houston Astrodome on September 20, 1973, for her highly anticipated match against Bobby Riggs, announcer Howard Cosell talked about subjects other than tennis. The 50 million viewers of the broadcast heard the legendary sportscaster discuss King's appearance. "[S]ometimes you get the feeling that if she ever let down her hair to her shoulders, took her glasses off, you'd have someone vying for a Hollywood screen test," he said on the air.[1]

Cosell was not focusing on King's athletic ability or her experience as a professional tennis player. But he, Riggs, and those watching the event would soon see King in fine form.

Playing Riggs

King would add the most famous accomplishment of her career that night. But it took much of the first set to establish her dominance. King took the first game with a

Responding to Cosell

When King heard Howard Cosell's description of her from the match against Riggs, she was fuming. She recalled her reaction: "I'm like, 'I don't want to be a movie star! I'm a jock; I'm an athlete! I love and have passion for what I do.' It's just horrible. He was talking about my looks! He didn't talk about one of my accomplishments."[2]

backhand volley winner. A few games later, Riggs broke King's serve to take a 3–2 lead. King stuck to the strategy she had decided on before the match: stay focused and make Riggs run. She hit the ball all over the court. The 55-year-old Riggs was forced to scurry for her shots. Before long, he was covered in sweat.

A tired Riggs began hitting weaker shots. King consistently placed her shots in corners and rushed to the net. When Riggs tried lobbing the ball over her head, King smashed them for winners. When he attempted to hit the ball past her, she tracked them down and angled the ball so he could not reach them.

After losing the first set, 6–4, Riggs recovered and broke King's serve. But King broke right back and took control again. The Astrodome crowd began feeling sorry for Riggs, who was starting to drag helplessly on the court, reaching in vain as King's forehands and backhands whizzed past him. The fans screamed encouragement, but King was merciless. She hit short shots to lure Riggs to the net, and then slammed the ball past him. At other times, she put Riggs away with volleys of her own. She won the second set 6–3.

Finishing Him Off

Riggs had entertained Americans with his sense of humor for months heading into the match, but he was not laughing now. His grim expression matched his feelings. He winced in pain as hand cramps set in midway through the third set. He plopped into his chair. The match was not done, but he was. And soon it was over. King tossed her racket into the air and smiled brightly.

Jack Kramer

Before her match against Riggs, King learned that old nemesis Jack Kramer would be a television commentator on the broadcast alongside Cosell. King strongly objected. She believed Kramer had stood in the way of the advancement of equitable pay for women players. She told network executives she would refuse to play if Kramer was allowed to go on the air. Kramer was forced to step aside, but not before stating he did so because he did not want King to use him as an excuse for losing to Riggs.

King watched her return to Riggs during their match in 1973.

She had avenged Court's loss with a 6–4, 6–3, 6–3 victory over Riggs.

The men's champion of an era gone by showed class in defeat by jumping over the net to congratulate King and whisper kindly in her ear that he had underestimated her. King patted Riggs on the back and sought out her husband. She nearly cried as she embraced him.

And when it was over, those who doubted King and the level of talent of the top female athletes doubted no more. Among those impressed was *Sports Illustrated* writer Curry Kirkpatrick, who wrote about the event:

> *On King's part it was a brilliant rising to an occasion; a clutch performance under the most trying of circumstances. Seldom has there been a more classic example of a skilled athlete performing at peak efficiency in the most important moment of her life.*
>
> *Because of Billie Jean alone, who was representing a sex supposedly unequipped for such things, what began as a huckster's hustle in defiance of serious athleticism ended up not mocking the game of tennis, but honoring it. This night King was both a shining piece of show biz and the essence of what sport is all about.[3]*

Best of Five

King knew she had to be in tremendous shape for her match against Riggs in 1973. One reason was that it was to be a best-of-five-sets match rather than a best-of-three match, which women played in tournaments. King knew she would have to run a lot and boast excellent endurance.

That night, millions also witnessed a woman who sat next to King during breaks and who shielded her from reporters after the match. Her name was Marilyn Barnett.

New Relationship

King had befriended Barnett, a Los Angeles, California, hairstylist, in the spring of 1972. King needed a friend outside the world of tennis and the media and quickly discovered that Barnett was someone with whom she could relax. King could enjoy

A Song about King

King's victory over Riggs proved inspirational to many people, including songwriter and singer Elton John. John, who was arguably the biggest star in pop music during the early 1970s, tracked King and her husband down in the locker room of the Denver Auditorium Arena in Colorado one day during the summer of 1974. The tennis star and the pop star met after her defeat of Riggs and had since become close friends.

Holding a tape recorder, she listened to a rough version of a song he had written and sung. Titled "Philadelphia Freedom,"

it was a tribute to King and the World TeamTennis team in Philadelphia, Pennsylvania, that King owned.

King was thrilled that John would write and record a song about her. She had met John at a party the year before and was so nervous she could not bring herself to approach him. He had felt the same way about her but finally summoned up the courage to speak to King.

John had always been her favorite recording artist. She was even more excited when "Philadelphia Freedom" rose to the top of the charts.

Barnett's company without having to discuss all the stresses in her life.

King knew she could be drawn to women as well as men. But she could hardly believe it when she began falling in love with Barnett. Though she questioned herself, she began to give in to the attraction. The two eventually started having an affair. King felt guilty about cheating on the husband she loved, but she felt confused about her feelings and the direction her personal life was headed.

Her feelings for Barnett seemed illogical to her because she remained deeply in love with Larry. Yet, she wanted Barnett by her side. King began paying Barnett $600 a month to be her personal assistant. Barnett traveled with the tennis star throughout 1973 and 1974. Barnett provided the media with quotes from and updates about King, who did little to hide Barnett from the public.

King soon regretted the relationship. She could not reveal that she was a lesbian because the media and the public would chastise her. At the time, people were far less accepting of homosexuals, especially among athletes.

Keeping her affair with Barnett a secret was maddening for the tennis star. And Barnett was showing signs of being quite controlling of King's time and emotions. King spoke of the relationship later:

The Two-Handed Backhand

Chris Evert and Jimmy Connors did more than change the sport of tennis with their immense talents. They also popularized the two-handed backhand. Almost all players held their rackets with one hand on their backhand strokes until Evert and Connors burst onto the tennis scene. Today, many professional players of both sexes use the two-handed backhand.

She was very possessive. She tried to control every day, each one more possessive and controlling. I started to realize what was happening. I had a feeling . . . I just didn't trust her. . . . She was a bad choice for me, but I was very vulnerable at the time we met. She was dangerous. I just screwed up.[4]

Most stressful to King was the thought that her parents would learn the truth. She knew her father disapproved of homosexuality. She fretted every moment that her relationship with Barnett would be revealed. King remained on her guard at all times. She looked to revive her marriage. Meanwhile, she continued focusing on tennis and helped to start a league that would bring tennis to the masses.

Marilyn Barnett

King, *left*, and other leaders of the women's movement passed a torch that was carried by foot from New York to Houston, Texas, for the November 1977 National Women's Convention.

The Organizer

King did a lot of soul-searching in the early 1970s. One fall day, she sat against a tree near Stinson Beach north of San Francisco, California. She asked herself why she needed to be in the spotlight.

After all, she had contemplated retiring from tennis earlier that year, but something continued to draw her back. She yearned to make a difference in the world and the sport, and she loved the game of tennis. King began to explore what she could do to improve life for her fellow female players. She decided that they still deserved more prize money as well as health benefits and solidarity as a group.

Fighting for Equality

King decided to organize a union. She invited 63 women to a conference in England. King's husband had already created bylaws for the union. After a great deal of discussion, the women agreed to them. The Women's Tennis Association was born. King was named its first president.

Next, King launched *womenSports* magazine and cofounded the Women's Sports Foundation in 1974. The nonprofit group was created to help female sports at the lower levels. Among its primary functions was to defend and expand Title IX, a bill signed by President Richard Nixon in 1972 that created college opportunities for women. King and others worked to ensure equal funding for women's high school and college academics and athletics.

Another Cause for King

Perhaps the most unusual problem faced by professional tennis officials revolved around a man who underwent an operation to become a woman. Richard Raskind was a graduate of Yale University. He later joined the US Navy, married, had children, and became an eye doctor.

While Raskind gave the appearance of being a typical guy, he was tormented by a feeling that he was a woman trapped in a man's body. As a result, Raskind divorced his wife, had a sex-change operation, and changed his name to Renée Richards.

A moderately successful tennis player as a male, Richards was good enough to compete professionally as a woman. She began entering events before the media discovered that the tall woman with the low voice was a transsexual. The United States Tennis Association promptly banned Richards from the 1976 US Open.

Richards took legal action. King supported her, saying, "If Renée thinks she is a woman in her heart and mind, then she is a woman."[1] When a judge on the New York State Supreme Court agreed, Richards played on the women's tour for a while, but with only limited success.

But King was forced to fight against more than the politicians who disagreed with Title IX. She was also challenged by some in the women's movement who claimed the legislation was not in their best interests. They believed sports were primarily a male activity that produced violence and a competitive nature that was unhealthy for women.

However, King and her supporters prevailed. In 1975, President Gerald Ford signed Title IX provisions into law that would ensure equal funding for men's and women's sports in high schools and colleges. It remains in place.

Title IX and College Football

College football coaches fervently opposed Title IX. Since football required the most funding, some coaches warned that the sport would be greatly damaged financially—even killed—by Title IX. The signing of Title IX into law, however, did not hurt college football. It remains as popular today as it did in the 1970s. It has continued to flourish financially as well.

World TeamTennis

King also examined how her match against Riggs had launched an era of tremendous popularity for tennis. Both she and her husband yearned to continue bringing tennis into the sports mainstream in the United States. So, they helped launch World TeamTennis (WTT) in 1974, making it a coed team sport. Franchises were placed in the largest US cities,

In December 1974, King, *left*, announced she would join ABC-TV as a commentator. Roone Arledge, president of ABC Sports, joined King at the conference.

including New York, Philadelphia, Chicago, and Los Angeles.

In tournament play, fans are continually reminded to keep quiet during points. But King loved the idea of her sport joining baseball, football, and basketball in encouraging yelling, screaming, and clapping during play. Thousands of fans turned out to watch their favorite stars compete in the WTT, including Rod Laver, Chris Evert, Jimmy Connors, and

Martina Navratilova. King played for and coached the Philadelphia Freedoms.

Another Singles Championship

King was so involved in WTT that she considered not playing the US Open in 1974. She had lost to the lesser skilled Olga Morozova two months earlier at Wimbledon and was tired. She finally made the decision to play.

Now in her early thirties, King continued to triumph on the court. She lost her No. 1 ranking to Evert in 1975 but remained masterful at Wimbledon, defeating Evert in the semifinals and Evonne Goolagong in the finals to secure her sixth championship in 15 years. Her three-set triumph over Goolagong was among King's proudest moments on a tennis court.

Retirement

Although 1975 brought King another Grand Slam

Tennis Court Surfaces

Tennis matches are played on three surfaces: grass, clay, and hard court. Since it is a fast surface, the players who hit with the most power boast an advantage on Wimbledon's grass courts. The French Open is the only Grand Slam tournament that is played on clay, which is the slowest surface. Those with the most consistent baseline strokes hit from the back of the court—often win that event. Most other events are played on hard surfaces, including the Australian and US Opens. Since its inception, the US Open is the only tournament to have been played on all three surfaces.

singles title, she announced her retirement following her US Open win. King retired from singles competition the following year. She needed knee surgery.

But King was not off the tennis court for long. The thrill of competition lured her back in 1977. King lost to Evert in the quarterfinals at Wimbledon, and it was becoming apparent that she was finally losing the skills that had made her the premier player in the world. King won no major singles or doubles events in 1978.

Making the year even more difficult was the collapse of WTT. While attendance had grown over the years and financial losses had decreased each season, the team owners had been discouraged by the lack of a network television contract and decided to disband.

While her tennis skills began to erode, she gained greater recognition for what she meant to women and to society off the court. In 1976, *Time* magazine selected King as one of its Women of the Year. And in 1977, *Harper's Bazaar* placed her on its 10 Most Powerful Women in America list. King had blossomed into one of the most admired women in the world. But her personal life was still filled with strife. And Marilyn Barnett would make it worse.

A First as a Coach

During the WTT's inaugural season, 1974, King coached the league's team in Philadelphia: the Philadelphia Freedoms. This role made King the first female coach of a team with male athletes.

In July 1975, King, *left*, joined Arthur Ashe on the dance floor in celebration of their singles victories at Wimbledon. It was King's sixth Wimbledon title.

CHAPTER 9

King, *right*, and Martina Navratilova posed after winning a doubles event.

Hanging Up Her Racket

As the 1970s drew to a close, players who never would have dreamed about beating King five years earlier were doing so regularly. King had lost her enthusiasm and many of her skills.

In 1979, she had teamed with the exceptional Martina Navratilova to win the Wimbledon women's doubles title—a record-breaking twentieth Wimbledon win. King had played regularly with Navratilova and expected to partner with her again at the famed All England Lawn Tennis Club in 1980. She was shocked to hear that Navratilova had teamed with Pam Shriver instead.

King waited for an explanation, but none came. Finally, she screamed at Navratilova, "You at least owe me this much—say something!" Navratilova walked past her without uttering a word. "Come on, Martina," King yelled. "[T]ell me I'm too old, tell me I can't play anymore, tell me I'm a gimp—anything—but tell me something."[1] Navratilova never said a word.

Serving Ritual

Just as basketball players often do the same things before every foul shot to stay in rhythm, tennis players use similar habits before they serve the ball. King always bounced the ball twice before tossing it in the air and hitting it. And if she felt tense or unfocused, she would repeat the ritual. She would also take four long, deep breaths to make certain she was relaxed.

Huge Loss

King faced other challenges during the early 1980s. Barnett had filed a lawsuit against King in May 1981. Barnett was seeking half of King's career earnings and a plush home in Malibu, California, that King had purchased for Barnett a month earlier to appease her. Barnett claimed to be a heartbroken woman who had given up her career for King.

King issued a press release stating that Barnett had been her secretary and that she had simply eliminated the position. But King knew she had to be more forthcoming with information about her relationship with Barnett. And with her ever-supportive husband and her parents by her side, King told a stunned audience in a nationally televised press conference that she had had an affair with Barnett that King had since ended. King then spoke about the relationship, which she described as a mistake.

King's admission of her affair with Barnett cost the tennis legend $1.5 million in endorsements over the next three years, including $500,000 from a Wimbledon clothing manufacturer and $300,000 from a jeans company. But she was not about to apologize. King had supported abortion rights and women's rights. Now, despite great criticism, she was supporting gay rights as well. King said of the situation:

> I don't feel homosexual. That's not my feelings, and I don't understand why people feel that I'm any less of a person.
>
> What they're saying is that it equals bad if someone happens to be homosexual. It's a fear, an unknown fear, and people don't understand it.[2]

Some people were sympathetic, including Los Angeles Superior Court Judge Julius Title. She dismissed Barnett's case, calling it an attempt at extortion. The judge ordered Barnett to leave the Malibu house.

The traumatic experience wreaked havoc with King's tennis game. In 1981, she lost to unknown Susie Rollinson in the first round of a tournament in Florida. And in 1982, King walked off the court during a match in Michigan. She could no longer simply go through

Billie Jean, *right*, leaned on Larry during a news conference in which she announced her relationship with Barnett.

the motions on the court. It pained her to play so poorly and without passion.

King searched her soul and realized that she did not want to quit. She fired herself up to play with enthusiasm. In 1982 and 1983, she managed to maintain a Top 20 spot in the women's rankings, which was not bad considering King was nearly 40 years old.

There were certainly financial reasons for King to continue competing on the professional tour. She yearned to make up the money lost in endorsements. Fellow players marveled at her performances despite two surgically repaired knees and that she was more than ten years older than the top women in the sport. Pam Shriver spoke highly of King's performance:

> You are sad for anyone who feels, for financial reasons,

Among the Most Important

King has received many awards from sports and news magazines. The latter were more noteworthy because they encompassed people from all walks of life, not only the athletic world. Among the most prestigious honors given to King occurred seven years after the completion of her playing career. In 1990, *Life* magazine placed her on its list of the 100 Most Important Americans of the 20th Century.

they have to keep going. But when you watched Billie Jean play, her spirit never deteriorated and her volleys never deteriorated. To this day, you see her volleys and shake your head. What she did in '82 and '83 was remarkable.[3]

Beginning of the End

The clock, however, was ticking on King's career. She became defensive when anyone suggested she retire. Athletes have often spoken about going out on their own terms and not being pitied for being a

Words of Wisdom

King has always been a bit of a philosopher. And though she has felt strongly about her opinions, particularly regarding women's equality, she has always attempted to respect the views of others. King wrote:

We do not live our lives in a vacuum. It is important to try to respect other people's positions, even if you disagree with them. Remember that their truth or perspective may not be the same as yours, and people sometimes make mistakes or are wrong—we all make mistakes.

At times, acting with integrity sometimes means practicing forgiveness, and learning how to ask for it. . . . So if you lie or mess up in some way, try to come clean and make things right again. But don't give up—always keep going, and keep trying to make better choices.[4]

King drew an analogy between tennis and that philosophy, adding that players see the results of every shot they make and can learn immediately what they did right or wrong. What is important is to learn from those mistakes on the court and to correct them.

shadow of their former selves. They generally know when their skills have deteriorated to the point where it is time for them to quit.

King experienced that moment at Wimbledon in 1983. She was ecstatic to reach the semifinals, but 18-year-old upstart Andrea Jaeger brought King crashing to earth by crushing her 6–1, 6–1. The 56-minute match was the most lopsided defeat for King in the 110 singles matches she had played during her career at Wimbledon.

As she departed Wimbledon, King gave the grass courts one last look, soaking in every detail. She wanted to remember it well because ten years after her thrilling victory over Riggs, King knew her career had come to an end.

King was done competing at that level in 1984, but she was

Loyal Supporter

The NBC television network hired King as an expert commentator on its Wimbledon broadcasts, but some wondered if she would be replaced in the wake of the Barnett incident. NBC did more than keep King. The network began using her for men's events as well. Though she lost many endorsements, King was grateful that NBC remained loyal.

not done fighting for women's equality and women's tennis. She also was not done finding herself. Though she had told the media that she did not feel that she was a homosexual, she would admit much later that she was simply fooling herself.

It would take another relationship with a woman, the painful experience of divorcing the man she still loved, and many years of emotional therapy to achieve what she had been trying to do for many years—be true to herself.

King, *right*, got through the court case against Barnett with the love and support of her husband.

CHAPTER 10

King at a book signing for *Pressure Is Privilege* in August 2008

True to Herself

King had a decision to make: accept who she was or give in to the pressures of society. The choice was not an easy one. Though she had begun a relationship with former doubles partner Ilana Kloss, King still had strong feelings for her husband. She had lost an estimated $1.5 million in endorsements since admitting her affair with Barnett and was fearful a repeat could cost her millions more.

So, while King's love for Kloss grew, so did her secrecy of their relationship. King claimed Kloss was merely a business partner. Meanwhile, she asked her husband for a divorce, but he refused. The couple lived apart, but he wanted to remain married. And King was too emotionally weak to end her marriage.

Finally, Kloss threatened to leave King if she did not get a divorce. In 1987, King finally summoned the courage to divorce the man who had helped her blossom as a person. In time, she nurtured her relationship with Kloss and spoke to mental health care professionals, which helped King embrace who she was. She expressed the changes she went through in a 2007 interview:

> For the whole time I was together with Marilyn [Barnett], I was overwhelmed with guilt. I felt guilty because I was brought up to believe that what I was doing was wrong in the eyes of God. I felt guilty because I was cheating on Larry. And I felt guilty because I knew that if it got out it could jeopardise [sic] the women's tour that was still in its infancy. I wasn't just in the closet, I was at the back of the closet hiding in the corner. . . . It was not until [I was] 51 that I fully accepted myself for who I am. I always understand rationally that there was nothing wrong with my sexuality, but it is not just about what you think but how you feel. It took 13 years of therapy to get me there, but I am glad I made it.[1]

Texting Sharapova

King sent young tennis champion Maria Sharapova text messages both before and after the 2008 Australian Open women's singles final. The first urged Sharapova to victory: "Champions take chances and pressure's a privilege."[2] The second congratulated her after a 7–5, 6–3 win over Ana Ivanovic. Sharapova quickly acknowledged how much hearing from the iconic King meant to her, noting the text messages during her post-match press conference.

King the Crusader

King became successful in many areas of her life. Following her playing career, she dedicated herself to the Women's Sports Foundation and helped create a new, scaled-down version of

WTT. In 1987, she was elected to the International Tennis Hall of Fame.

King continued to make an impact on the sport as a coach as well. She made amends with Navratilova and took the champion under her wing. Navratilova had begun to slip by 1990, but King revamped her game and made it stronger.

In the early 1990s, King furthered the cause of coed athletics by investing in Discovery Zone play centers for young children. Her motivation was to get kids of both sexes playing together without thought to gender and to foster self-esteem in girls and boys alike.

Changing Times

King had always been a crusader for women and her sport both as a professional athlete and following her retirement from the sport. She was disappointed in later years by the lack of awareness of today's female athletes about the battles that took place in the past for which they have reaped the benefits. She also expressed disappointment that many of today's women sports stars are not actively improving the lot for future female athletes.

King cited an interview with tennis star Jennifer Capriati, who responded to a question about Title IX by stating she had no idea what it was. King noted that the modern athletes make so much money that they no longer consider putting their careers or reputations on the line to fight a moral battle. King explained:

There's no pain. The girls make so much money; the boys make so much money. There's not enough pain. You've got to have some pain to change things, and, I think, to grow. They always want things so much better, which is good, but you know what? There's only a few people who drive it.[3]

In 1995, at the age of 52, King took over as captain of the US Federation Cup team. The Federation Cup is an international women's team tennis competition. A year later, she guided the US team to a victory over Spain. She also coached American tennis players to medal-winning victories in multiple Olympic Games.

Another triumph was one over an eating disorder that developed later in her life. King began binge eating as a kid, but it spiraled out of control as she strove to find her sexual identity. She overcame the disorder but faced a new challenge in her sixties when she was diagnosed with type 2 diabetes. King learned to manage that disease. And, as has become her fashion, King led a charge to raise awareness of diabetes as the spokesperson for the Face of Change campaign.

Goodbye to Bobby

One of the more touching moments of King's later life revolved around her relationship with Riggs. She learned she had a great deal in common with him.

The once proud and vibrant man was diagnosed with prostate cancer for the second time in 1995, the year his wife died. Riggs became despondent but grew to understand what his match against King meant to the United States. It was not simply his finest hustle. It was a triumph for American women and an awakening for the nation to the righteousness of equality.

President Barack Obama presented the 2009 Presidential Medal of Freedom to King for her contribution to US culture. It is the highest civilian honor in the United States.

King taught Riggs that through countless conversations. The two became friends. She wanted Riggs to understand he had participated in a monumental event that transcended sports. In 1995, King learned that Riggs was dying. During a telephone conversation, she asked Riggs if she could visit him, but he refused. He did not want her to see him in such a sickly state. On October 25, she called again.

"I love you," she told him.

"I love you," he replied. Then he added, "Well,

The USTA Honors King

In August 2006, the United States Tennis Association (USTA) paid tribute to King by renaming its national headquarters in her honor: USTA Billie Jean King National Tennis Center. Sportscaster and former professional tennis player Mary Carillo said of King at the event, "She's for the rich, the poor, black, white, straight, gay, she wants equality for everyone. She's not just a great tennis player and a women's libber, and that's an important thing to keep in mind."[5]

we did it. We really made a difference, didn't we?"[4]

King certainly has—on and off the court. Though her greatest personal triumph was bravely leading the charge for equality for women's tennis, her most far-reaching impact was through her role in making Title IX a reality. The bill signed into law in 1975 allowed girls everywhere to realize their athletic potential. It provided an opportunity for women's college sports and athletes to thrive. Before Title IX, girls' high school sports were virtually nonexistent. Today, they are as much a part of the school landscape as those involving males.

Billie Jean King continues to work to promote the sport she loves. She is cherished and remembered for the impact she has had on the United States and on the women's movement. The brilliance she displayed on the tennis court as well as her leadership as a humanitarian gave her a chance to change her country.

King found fame as a tennis player and used her fame to fight for the rights of others.

1943

Billie Jean Moffitt is born in Long Beach, California, on November 22.

1954

Moffitt takes her first tennis lessons.

1959–1960

Moffitt plays on the American Junior Wightman team.

1965

Moffitt marries Larry King on September 17 and becomes Billie Jean King.

1966

King wins her first Wimbledon singles title in July.

1967

King wins singles titles at Wimbledon and the US national tournament.

1961

Moffitt teams with Karen Hantze to win her first Wimbledon's doubles title in July; Moffitt begins attending college in the fall.

1962

Moffitt repeats her doubles victory at Wimbledon.

1964

Moffitt works in Australia with instructor Mervyn Rose, who transforms her game.

1968

King helps end the amateur system by signing a professional contract with the National Tennis League; King undergoes her first knee surgery.

1970

King organizes a tournament boycott that leads to formation of the Virginia Slims tour and the Women's Tennis Association.

1971

King wins the US Open women's singles championship.

1972

A campaign spearheaded by King and others results in the passage of Title IX. She wins three Grand Slam events.

1972

King begins a relationship with hairdresser Marilyn Barnett.

1973

King defeats Bobby Riggs in the Battle of the Sexes on September 20.

1981

A lawsuit by Barnett forces King to admit to a homosexual affair. A judge dismisses the suit, but King loses $1.5 million in endorsements.

1984

King retires from tennis at age 40 after reaching the Wimbledon semifinals the previous two years.

1987

King divorces her husband. She is elected to the International Tennis Hall of Fame.

1974

King and her husband launch World TeamTennis with franchises in 16 major US cities.

1978

King suffers through tough times. She wins no major tournaments and sees World TeamTennis fold.

1979

King wins the Wimbledon women's doubles title in July.

1990

King begins coaching Martina Navratilova. *Life* magazine selects King as one of the 100 Most Important Americans of the 20th Century.

1995

King takes over as coach of the US Federation Cup team.

2006

The US Tennis Association renames the site of the US Open the Billie Jean King USTA National Tennis Center.

ESSENTIAL FACTS

DATE OF BIRTH
November 22, 1943

PLACE OF BIRTH
Long Beach, California

PARENTS
Bill and Betty Moffitt

EDUCATION
Long Beach Polytechnic High School
Los Angeles State College

MARRIAGE
Larry King (1965–1987)

CAREER HIGHLIGHTS
Billie Jean King's talent as a tennis player emerged while she was a teenager, when she was asked to be part of the American Junior Wightman team in 1959 and 1960. She won her first Wimbledon title in women's doubles in 1961. Five years later, King won the first of her six Wimbledon singles titles. The following year, she won the US national event, which would soon become the US Open, a tournament she would ultimately win four times. In 1970, King led several fellow players in a tournament boycott that resulted in the Virginia Slims tour and the Women's Tennis Association. In 1973, King played Bobby Riggs in the Battle of the Sexes. The following year, King and her husband founded World TeamTennis. After retiring in 1984, King became a coach.

SOCIETAL CONTRIBUTION

As a player, King fought for equality for women tennis players. King's defeat of Riggs helped show that women are as talented and as able as men. King has used her celebrity to fight for equality off the court as well. She spearheaded an effort to implement Title IX, ensuring equality of funding of women's amateur athletics. She has been a proponent of all people, encouraging acceptance and equal treatment of everyone. King's work on and off the court has garnered attention throughout the years, including being named Sportswoman of the Year in 1972 by *Sports Illustrated* and listed as one of the 100 Most Important Americans of the 20th Century in 1990 by *Life*.

CONFLICTS

Growing up in an era when women were often thought of as inferior to men and held to roles now considered traditional, King experienced discrimination as a female tennis player. She used her status to fight for women's equality on and off the tennis court. In her personal life, she was challenged legally by Marilyn Barnett, a woman with whom King had an affair. Publicizing the affair cost King $1.5 million in endorsements. The relationship challenged King psychologically as she struggled with coming to terms and dealing with her sexuality.

QUOTE

"We do not live our lives in a vacuum. It is important to try to respect other people's positions, even if you disagree with them. Remember that their truth or perspective may not be the same as yours, and people sometimes make mistakes or are wrong—we all make mistakes. At times, acting with integrity sometimes means practicing forgiveness, and learning how to ask for it. . . . So if you lie or mess up in some way, try to come clean and make things right again. But don't give up—always keep going, and keep trying to make better choices."
—*Billie Jean King,* Pressure Is Privilege

GLOSSARY

abortion
A medical procedure that ends a pregnancy.

amateur
Someone who competes without being paid.

athletic scholarship
Tuition and other money provided to talented athletes to play for a particular college's team.

backhand
A tennis stroke in which a player reaches across the body to hit the ball.

championship
The final match of a tournament that determines the winner of the event.

court
A surface on which a tennis match is played, including the net.

doubles
A match played between two pairs of players.

forehand
A tennis stroke on the same side of the body as the hand holding the racket.

Grand Slam
The four major annual events for male and female tennis players: the Australian Open, the French Open, Wimbledon, and the US Open.

homosexual
A person who is most sexually and emotionally attracted to those of the same sex.

lob

A tennis shot placed over the head of a player who has moved up to or is at the net.

match

A series of sets to determine the winner of a tennis competition between players.

serve

The opening of a point in tennis in which a player tosses the ball in the air and must hit it into a defined area on the opponent's side of the court.

set

Part of a match won by the player who wins six games first; sometimes more, because one must win by at least two games.

singles

A match played between two players.

Title IX

The 1972 bill signed into law three years later that ensured equality in funding for girls' and women's amateur athletics.

tournament

A tennis event involving a number of players in which the winners continue to advance until one player in the event is left as champion.

volley

A shot struck while the ball is in the air, usually near the net, generally intended to clinch a point.

SELECTED BIBLIOGRAPHY

DeFord, Frank, and King, Billie Jean. *Billie Jean.* New York: Viking, 1982. Print.

King, Billie Jean. *Pressure Is a Privilege: Lessons I've Learned from Life and the Battle of the Sexes.* New York: LifeTime Media, 2008. Print.

Roberts, Selena. *A Necessary Spectacle: Billie Jean King, Bobby Riggs, and the Tennis Match That Leveled the Game.* New York: Crown, 2005. Print.

FURTHER READING

Blumenthal, Karen. *Let Me Play: The Story of Title IX: The Law That Changed the Future of Girls in America.* New York: Atheneum, 2005. Print.

Grosser, Manfred, and Richard Schonborn. *Competitive Tennis for Young Players: The Road to Becoming a Top Player.* Aachen, Germany: Meyer & Meyer Sports, 2002. Print.

WEB LINKS

To learn more about Billie Jean King, visit ABDO Publishing Company online at **www.abdopublishing.com**. Web sites about Billie Jean King are featured on our Book Links page. These links are routinely monitored and updated to provide the most current information available.

PLACES TO VISIT

For more information on this subject, contact or visit the following organizations.

International Tennis Hall of Fame
194 Bellevue Avenue, Newport, RI 02840
401-849-3990
www.tennisfame.com
This museum gives an overview of the history of tennis. It features interactive exhibits, videos, and memorabilia from legendary champions to current superstars. Enshrinee Hall commemorates the premier players who have been inducted into the Hall of Fame.

USTA Billie Jean King National Tennis Center
Flushing Meadow/Corona Park, Flushing, NY 11368
718-760-6200
www.usta.com/USTA/Global/About_Us/USTA_Billie_Jean_King_National_Tennis_Center/Information/14191 USTA Billie_Jean_King_National_Tennis_Center_Information.aspx
The site of the annual US Open since 1978, it is the largest public tennis facility in the world. Visit the Arthur Ashe Stadium, where the championship matches are held every year.

World TeamTennis
1776 Broadway, Suite 600, New York, NY 10019
212-586-3444
www.wtt.com
Visit World TeamTennis's Web site for information about this professional tennis league created by Billie Jean and Larry King. The site includes information about recreational leagues as well, which were created in 1985 and now involve nearly 500,000 amateur players in the United States.

SOURCE NOTES

CHAPTER 1: The Mother's Day Massacre

1. Selena Roberts. *A Necessary Spectacle: Billie Jean King, Bobby Riggs, and the Tennis Match That Leveled the Game.* New York: Crown, 2005. 16. Print.

2. Ibid.

3. Ibid. 10.

4. Curry Kirkpatrick. *"A Mother's Day Ms. Match."* SI.com. Time Warner, 21 May 1973. Web. 29 Oct. 2009.

CHAPTER 2: California Tomboy

1. Billie Jean King. *Pressure is a Privilege: Lessons I've Learned from Life and the Battle of the Sexes.* New York: LifeTime Media, 2008. 36–37. Print.

2. Chris McKendry: "Thank You, Billie Jean," *ESPN.com.* ESPN Internet Ventures, 2007. Web. 14 Oct. 2010.

3. Billie Jean King with Frank DeFord. *Billie Jean.* New York: Viking, 1982. 73. Print.

4. June Thomas. "Billie Jean King." *Slate.com.* Washington Post.Newsweek Interactive, 30 Aug. 2006. Web. 14 Oct. 2010.

5. Chris McKendry: "Thank You, Billie Jean," ESPN.com. ESPN Internet Ventures. 2007. Web. 6 Aug. 2010.

CHAPTER 3. Marble, Wimbledon, and College

1. Selena Roberts. *A Necessary Spectacle: Billie Jean King, Bobby Riggs, and the Tennis Match That Leveled the Game.* New York: Crown, 2005. 60. Print.

2. Ibid. 57.

CHAPTER 4. Finding Love

1. Selena Roberts. *A Necessary Spectacle: Billie Jean King, Bobby Riggs, and the Tennis Match That Leveled the Game.* New York: Crown, 2005. 61. Print.

2. Ibid. 62.

CHAPTER 5. Taking a Stand

1. Selena Roberts. *A Necessary Spectacle: Billie Jean King, Bobby Riggs, and the Tennis Match That Leveled the Game.* New York: Crown, 2005. 75. Print.

2. Roy Blount. "More Joan of Arc Than Shirley Temple." *SI.com.* Time Warner, 20 Sept. 1971. Web. 29 Nov. 2009.

CHAPTER 6. Wanted and Unwanted Attention

1. Billie Jean King. *Pressure Is a Privilege: Lessons I've Learned from Life and the Battle of the Sexes.* New York: LifeTime Media, 2008. 41. Print.

CHAPTER 7. Career High and Personal Low

1. Jay Lovinger. *The Gospel According to ESPN: Saints, Saviors & Sinners.* New York: Hyperion, 2002. 54. Print.

2. Selena Roberts. *A Necessary Spectacle: Billie Jean King, Bobby Riggs, and the Tennis Match That Leveled the Game.* New York: Crown, 2005. 149. Print.

3. Curry Kirkpatrick, "There She Is, Ms. America," *SI.com.* Time Warner, 1 Oct. 1973. Web. 14 Oct. 2010.

4. Selena Roberts. *A Necessary Spectacle: Billie Jean King, Bobby Riggs, and the Tennis Match That Leveled the Game.* New York: Crown, 2005. 120–121. Print.

CHAPTER 8. The Organizer

1. Selena Roberts. *A Necessary Spectacle: Billie Jean King, Bobby Riggs, and the Tennis Match That Leveled the Game.* New York: Crown, 2005. 166. Print.

CHAPTER 9. Hanging Up Her Racket

1. Billie Jean King with Frank DeFord. *Billie Jean.* New York: Viking, 1982. 193. Print.

2. Selena Roberts. *A Necessary Spectacle: Billie Jean King, Bobby Riggs, and the Tennis Match That Leveled the Game.* New York: Crown, 2005. 177. Print.

3. Ibid. 239.

4. Billie Jean King. *Pressure Is a Privilege: Lessons I've Learned from Life and the Battle of the Sexes.* New York: LifeTime Media, 2008. 151. Print.

CHAPTER 10. True to Herself

1. Matthew Syed. "Fight against discrimination goes on for the reluctant revolutionary." *TimesOnline*. Times Newspapers, 14 Sept. 2007. Web. 14 Oct. 2010.

2. Grant Clark and Heidi Couch. "Perspective, Billie Jean's Text Lift Sharapova to Third Major." *Bloomberg.com*. Bloomberg, 26 Jan. 2008. Web. 14 Oct. 2010.

3. Selena Roberts. *A Necessary Spectacle: Billie Jean King, Bobby Riggs, and the Tennis Match That Leveled the Game.* New York: Crown, 2005. 229. Print.

4. Ibid. 251–252.

5. June Thomas. "Billie Jean King." *Slate.com*. Washington Post.Newsweek Interactive, 30 Aug. 2006. Web. 14 Oct. 2010.

INDEX

ABOUT THE AUTHOR

Marty Gitlin is a freelance writer who has written more than 20 educational books, many of them about sports topics. Gitlin has won more than 45 awards during his 25 years as a writer, including first place for general excellence from the Associated Press. He lives with his wife and three children in Ohio.

PHOTO CREDITS